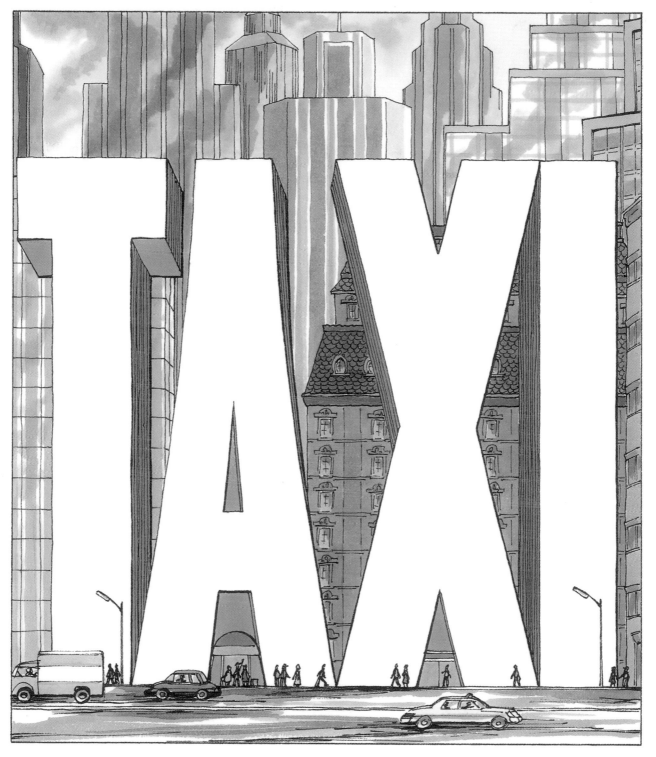

A BOOK OF CITY WORDS BY BETSY & GIULIO MAESTRO

CLARION BOOKS
NEW YORK

Clarion Books
a Houghton Mifflin Company imprint
52 Vanderbilt Avenue, New York, NY 10017
Text copyright © 1989 by Betsy Maestro
Illustrations copyright © 1989 by Giulio Maestro
All rights reserved.
For information about permission to reproduce
selections from this book, write to Permissions,
Houghton Mifflin Company, 2 Park Street, Boston, MA 02108.
Printed in the USA

Library of Congress Cataloging-in-Publication Data
Maestro, Betsy.
    Taxi: a book of city words/by Betsy Maestro; illustrated by
Giulio Maestro.
        p.   cm.
    Summary: The reader is introduced to such typical city words as
"theater," "museum," "office building," and "train station" as a taxi
travels through a hectic workday in and around the city.
    ISBN 0-89919-528-8
    1. Vocabulary – Juvenile literature.   2. City and town life –
Juvenile literature.   [1. Vocabulary.   2. City and town life.]
I. Maestro, Giulio, ill.   II. Title.
PE1449.M325 1989
428.1 – dc19   88-22867
                        CIP
                        AC

Y   10 9 8 7 6 5 4 3 2 1

It is morning in the **city**. Another busy day is beginning.

The yellow **taxi** drives out to work. It will pick up many passengers today.

A **train** is running high above as the taxi moves quickly along.

The taxi stops at a tall **office building**. The people who get in are in a hurry.

"We have a train to catch," they say. "We can't be late!" The taxi rushes them to the **railroad station**.

At a big **apartment house**, a family climbs into the
waiting taxi.

When the taxi stops at the **zoo**, the children dash off to see the animals.

Then the taxi picks up a man and a woman. They have to meet a **cruise ship** that has just docked.

The taxi takes them to the crowded **pier**. The man and the woman step out, and passengers from the ship get in.

These people live across the river, outside the city.
The taxi drives over the **bridge** to take them home.

The taxi comes back through a **tunnel** that goes
under the river.

As it enters the city again, the taxi drives by the **police station**.

In front of a very tall **skyscraper**, a young woman is waiting. When the taxi stops, she jumps in.

"Hurry!" she says, "My plane is leaving soon." The taxi gets her to the **airport** as fast as it can.

Now the taxi takes the **highway** back to the city.
Along the way, the driver stops for gas.

Soon the taxi is in the city again. It is lunchtime and the driver is hungry. At a **coffee shop**, he parks the taxi and grabs a quick meal.

The first stop after lunch is at a fancy **hotel**. The taxi's new passengers are visiting the city.

They have tickets for a show. The taxi lets them out in front of the **theater**.

The taxi drives up the narrow **street**. Cars are
double-parked, so it is hard to get through.

The taxi turns onto a wide **avenue**. It is not as crowded here. Many taxis are hurrying along.

At a **museum**, another family crowds into the taxi.
It is a tight squeeze, but the ride will be short.

The family is going to shop at a large **department store**. The taxi pulls up in front.

At the **hospital**, three more people are waiting. The taxi stops to pick them up. They live close by.

In a few minutes, the people are home. The taxi turns around and drives slowly through the **park**.

It is getting dark now in the city. Near a **newsstand**, the driver sees a couple waiting.

The man and the woman are going to a **restaurant** across town for dinner. The taxi takes them there.

On the way back, the taxi stops at its last **traffic light** of the day. When the light turns green, the taxi heads home.

It is getting late and the driver is tired. At the
firehouse, the taxi makes a turn.

It is back at the **garage**. This is the end of a very busy day. In the morning, all over the city, more people will be waiting for the yellow taxi.

About the Author

Betsy Maestro taught kindergarten and first grade for eleven years and earned a Masters Degree in Elementary Guidance. Since 1974, she has been collaborating with her husband, Giulio, on concept books for young children, including the popular *Harriet* series. They have also created *The Story of the Statue of Liberty* and *A More Perfect Union*, an ALA Notable Book. *Taxi* is Ms. Maestro's first book for Clarion.

About the Artist

Giulio Maestro attended the Cooper Union Art School and worked for several years in advertising. He has been illustrating and writing children's books since 1969. Mr. Maestro has illustrated many of Clarion's word play books, including four of his own, *Riddle Romp*, *Razzle-Dazzle Riddles*, *What's Mite Might?*, and *What's a Frank Frank?*

The Maestros live in Old Lyme, Connecticut, with their two children, Daniela and Marco.